Daily Agreements, Guidelines & Intentions

A simple plan to create what comes next

Written by:

Aimee Mosco and Donald L. Ferguson

Co-owners of Intentional Healing Systems, LLC.

Intentional Healing Systems, LLC
www.ihsunity.com

Cover design and interior formatting by Tugboat Design
Cover art and interior art contributions by Leon van Kraayenburg

Contents

Introduction

What if we were able to harness a greater portion of our mind's potential by directing more of the activity that goes on in our brain? What if we could consciously program our subconscious to carry out an intricate list of thoughtful directives on a daily basis to inspire our actions?

We can. And this book gives you some very simple tools to accomplish the task at will.

Most people are familiar with phrases like "Mind over matter" and "You can do anything you set your mind to." We tend to remember these phrases when we are faced with challenges, are looking for solutions, or are driven to meet particular goals. Using or planning our thoughts to inspire action and dictate how the journey of life goes is something that we generally call upon as a secondary measure.

Many of us have instituted belief systems that were indoctrinated in us beginning with our first breath after birth. They were absolutely appropriate for levels of awareness experienced by our ancestors, but we have grown by leaps and bounds and it has come time for us to adjust our beliefs to support our endeavors as powerful creative beings.

We are driven to act by our beliefs. When we consciously manage belief structures, we put ourselves in charge of outcomes rather than at the mercy of them.

What this means is that deciding to use the techniques in this book doesn't have to coincide with desperation. The strategies in this book don't have to be a counter-measure to failure. They don't have to act as a remedy for something—an event, a relationship, or a major change--that tests a person's will. They can be a daily practice, a preemptive measure, and a choice to facilitate smoother navigation of life.

Delegating Thoughts

> *"We have to dream in order to survive."*
> —*Dr. Beverly Crusher (Gates McFadden),*
> *"Star Trek: The Next Generation"*

Did you know your mind never sleeps? As long as your blood is flowing, some part of your mind is in motion. This is part of why we dream. Our mind gives us all kinds of information about our hopes, fears, desires and struggles through our dreams. Several books have been written on this, but your mind also gives you information and subtle cues while you are awake—even when you think you are just vegging or daydreaming.

Human beings have developed mechanisms to suppress awareness of what goes on in our brains because it would be overwhelming to consciously track our mind's activity. This does not translate to having no control over what transpires when we are not fully aware. Much research has been done on the role our subconscious plays. It functions as a way to help us make judgments about people and situations (sometimes wrong) and operate smoothly without our executive functions—our higher reasoning and decision making—being overwhelmed. If you've ever had the feeling that you didn't want to have lunch with someone and you couldn't explain why, now you know! Your subconscious helped you spend your time in a better way.

While most of us do not engage in the practice of consciously delegating thoughts and focus to the subconscious mind, we have the absolute ability to do so.

One way to do this is to plan.

If you map out directives and general thought patterns that promote success, you can transfer this information to your subconscious at will, with ease and repetition. It is simple to do and begins with general, but meaningful, direction. As you become accustomed to directing your subconscious, your personal creation process becomes more intentional. Once you have laid the foundation for new outcomes with your subconscious thought patterns, you can then identify specific goals you want to achieve, visualize success, and take action to meet those goals. The agreements, guidelines and intentions in this book address general objectives and are meant to help streamline and support your personal creation process.

Collective Body of Information

> *"I like to think (and*
> *the sooner the better!)*
> *of a cybernetic meadow*
> *where mammals and computers*
> *live together in mutually*
> *programming harmony*
> *like pure water*
> *touching clear sky."*
> —*Richard Brautigan (via AllPoetry.com)*

A body of information that we all have access to connects humans. Some call it the universe with a capital U, while others call it the collective consciousness. We refer to it as a collective (or unified) body of information. This body of information is in a perpetual state of expansion as humanity evolves. It can easily be compared to the Internet because it functions similarly, only it is much more finely tuned.

You can use your connection to the Internet to procure and share volumes of information. We have learned through our own mistakes, and the mistakes of others, that it is wise to use discernment when we share information on the Internet because the audience is so vast, and information travels instantaneously. Once we post something it is fair game for anyone with an Internet connection to look at and pass judgment on, and it stays in cyberspace forever in some form. On the constructive front, if we have an important message to share and are looking for support, the Internet is an invaluable tool to distribute our request for support far and wide.

Similarly, the collective body of information responds to the subtle emissions of the human energy field—think of them as texts, Facebook likes, tweets, YouTube videos and Internet comments. Our subconscious mind posts our personal energy field emanations daily, generally without discernment, and can be even more disruptive in our lives than a tweet written in anger.

This book is meant to act as a training tool for managing subtle subconscious emissions. You will learn how to distribute emanations from your energy field to the collective body of information in a calculated manner as you read on.

The Internet has "Terms of Service" and online communities have codes of conduct. The agreements, guidelines and intentions outlined in this book act as those codes, so to speak, and as subconscious emanations programming to either fortify the collective body of information in efforts to heal the planet we all share, or to ask for collective support by stating expectations in relationship to personal goals. Either way is a win for collective humanity and fortification for our IHS concept of Unity among all living beings.

Agreements, Guidelines and Intentions

The agreements, guidelines and intentions laid out in this book are suggested directives to transfer to your subconscious.

The **agreements** state your commitment to an underlying focus.

The **guidelines** dictate general expectations of how information is to be relayed to, from and through you. Guidelines help to remove obstacles before they are given the chance to be erected.

The **intentions** function as a practical application of the Law of Attraction (popularized by "The Secret"). The expression of intentions draws energetic components toward you needed to narrow your focus. Focus is what inspires actions that nurture and support manifestation.

We suggest that you exercise your creativity to customize these documents. We've created space for you to add line items to the suggested agreements, guidelines and intentions. Your additions should speak to your underlying focus and subconscious thought patterns that inspire actions supporting achievement of your personal goals.

If you choose not to alter the agreements, guidelines and intentions, that is OK too. The general directives in each document support favorable focus and it is not imperative that you assign any more specifics for them to benefit you. However, it is important to understand that your input only makes these tools more effective for you. Connecting with and integrating the information in these altered or un-altered agreements, guidelines and intentions, make you an active participant in shaping your journey going forward.

Creating Personal Goals

"Life's altered you, as it's altered me.
And what would be the point of living if it didn't change us?"
—Charles Earnest Carson (*Jim Carter*), *"Downton Abbey"*

Creating personal goals in connection with integrating the underlying focus outlined in the agreements, guidelines and intentions is very important. Your goals act as a road map to new outcomes. They allow you to set your sights on what it is that you want to create in your life. Your manifested goals are the intentional product of your personal creation process.

Your goals are highly personal and specific to you. There are no limitations. We provide suggested uses for the agreements, guidelines and sets of intentions outlined in this book, but we recommend that you take some time and create a personal goal for each of the documents that speak to you. Write them down with the current date on the worksheets provided in this book or on a separate piece of paper. Committing yourself to your goals sets the wheels of change in motion in a very directed manner.

You will find that your goals will change as you change and grow, so we recommend that you revisit your goals periodically and adjust them accordingly.

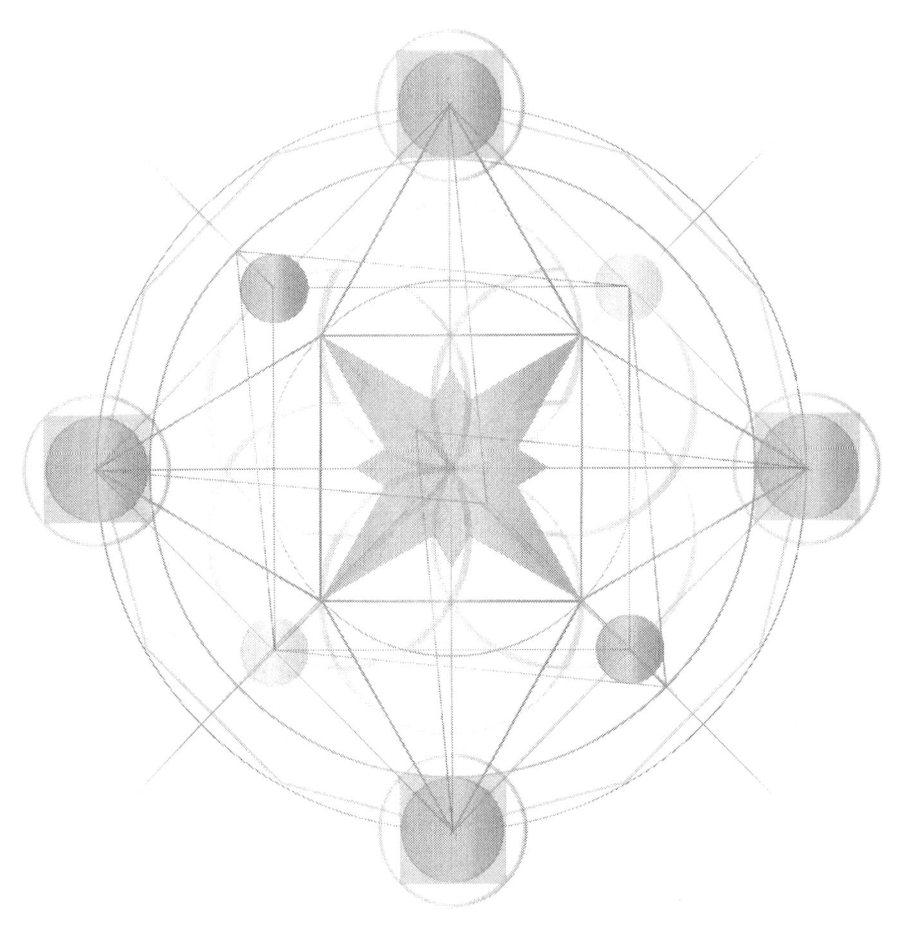

Components of the Creation Process

Contrary to pop psychology, there is no shortcut for intentionally "creating". You must have some level of active and conscious participation in order to achieve what you set out to create. The bridge (or roadblock) between your intended goals and your manifested goals is what you DO to partake in the achievement of them. The actions you take and choose to engage in will be greatly influenced by your subconscious focus.

The process outlined in this book acts as an alignment tool for your conscious and subconscious thoughts. Your subconscious thought patterns hold your underlying focus steady while your conscious mind focuses on the goals you have set. The alignment created between the two can thwart unintentional self-sabotage.

Sometimes it is difficult to know what actions will support your success. For example, you could be invited to two equally desirable events on the same night and time. Which one supports your goals? Perhaps you can arrange to attend both if you determine that both fulfill you in some way. Arrive early at one event so you can leave earlier, then attend the second one later.

As you streamline your personal creation process by bringing the subconscious and conscious components of yourself together to work in a calculated, intentional and harmonious way, you will effectively be guiding yourself toward taking supportive actions.

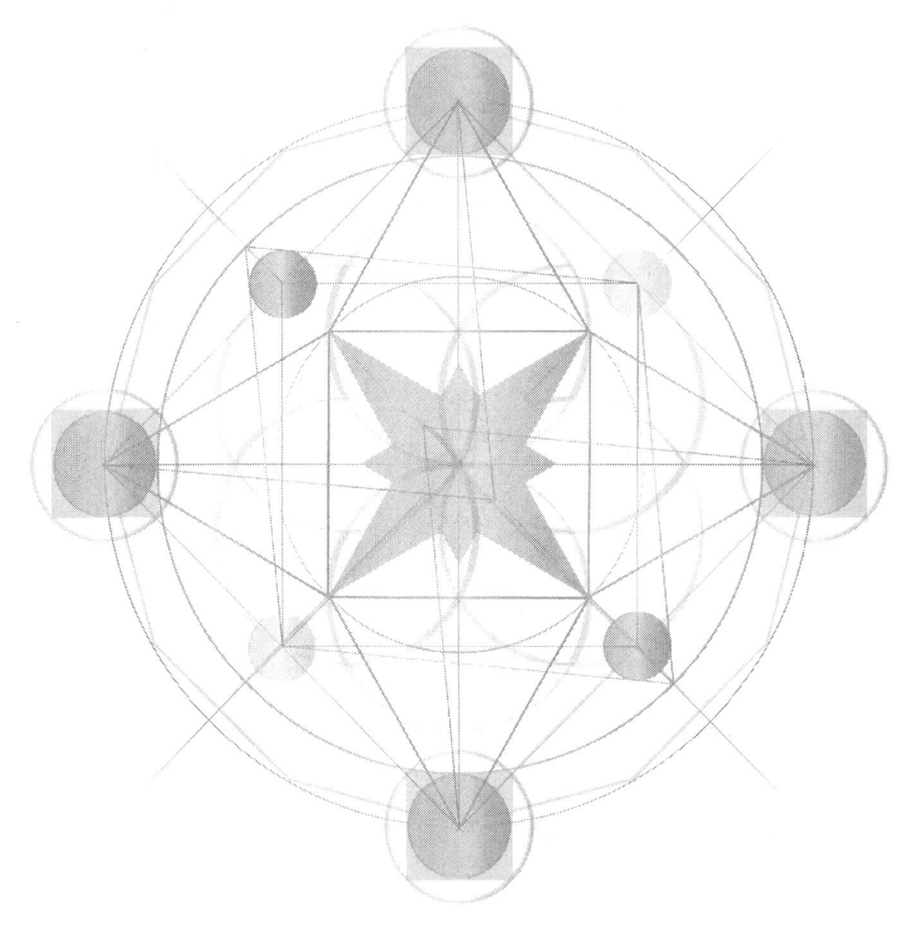

Symbols

"One of the things you do as a writer and as a filmmaker is grasp for resonant symbols and imagery without necessarily fully understanding it yourself."
—*Christopher Nolan, director*

Symbols have been used throughout the ages as associative references. In Ancient Egypt, hieroglyphics were symbols used to tell stories as well as a means of documenting Egyptian life. In modern times, companies use symbols as logos to identify and distinguish themselves in a condensed manner. Some of these may have their basis in ancient symbols that we all know in the collective consciousness. It is no secret that a picture really is worth 1000 words—think of emojis!

Thanks to the presence of commerce and technology, people from around the world and from every background can identify with how powerful and effective symbols are. Imagine you are driving down the freeway and you see a billboard displaying the logo of a commonly known fast food restaurant chain you have eaten at. That logo summons recollection of a wealth of associations. You instantly connect with menu items, the containers the food is served in, greetings used by the employees, commonalities in different locations such as restaurant layout, reviews and reports of company statistics, the good service you had at those eateries, and so on. Those are just the things brought to the forefront of your consciousness. Your subconscious is producing recall of more intricate details such as the taste of the fries and the smell of the grease on your hands after you have finished eating. You are not likely focusing on this information on a daily basis, but seeing the logo, or company symbol, allows for all of this information to be brought back into focus.

The symbols found in this book function in a similar way to modern day company logos. Each symbol is associated with intricate information outlined in a corresponding agreement, set of guidelines, list of intentions and optional personal specifications. Once you have read the corresponding text, created personal specifications and associated the symbol with that information, you can call that information forth just by connecting with the symbol.

Affirmations

Affirmations serve as tools to train your brain to believe that an outcome has either come to fruition or is imminent. They are an important element of manifestation because they infuse belief and set clear parameters for actions to create outcomes.

The **agreements, guidelines, intentions and corresponding symbols** in this book are paired with general affirmations in an effort to connect you with the practice of subconscious focus and build confidence through belief. When you ask to recall and delegate the details of the documents through visual connection with the symbol, you protect and strengthen the effectiveness of the directives by expressing the designated affirmation. What this means is that through affirmations, through saying, "I AM," you are sending a message through all parts of your conscious and sub-conscious mind to reinforce your convicted belief that you are producing new outcomes. Your belief breathes the life into what it is that you are creating.

The energy of your beliefs emanate from your energy field, detailing your expectations and communicating them to the collective body of information. They become exponentially more powerful once you share them, effectively asking for help and support in your achievement of them.

As stated, the affirmations assigned to each symbol in this book are general, but they still speak effectively to the achievement of many different personal goals.

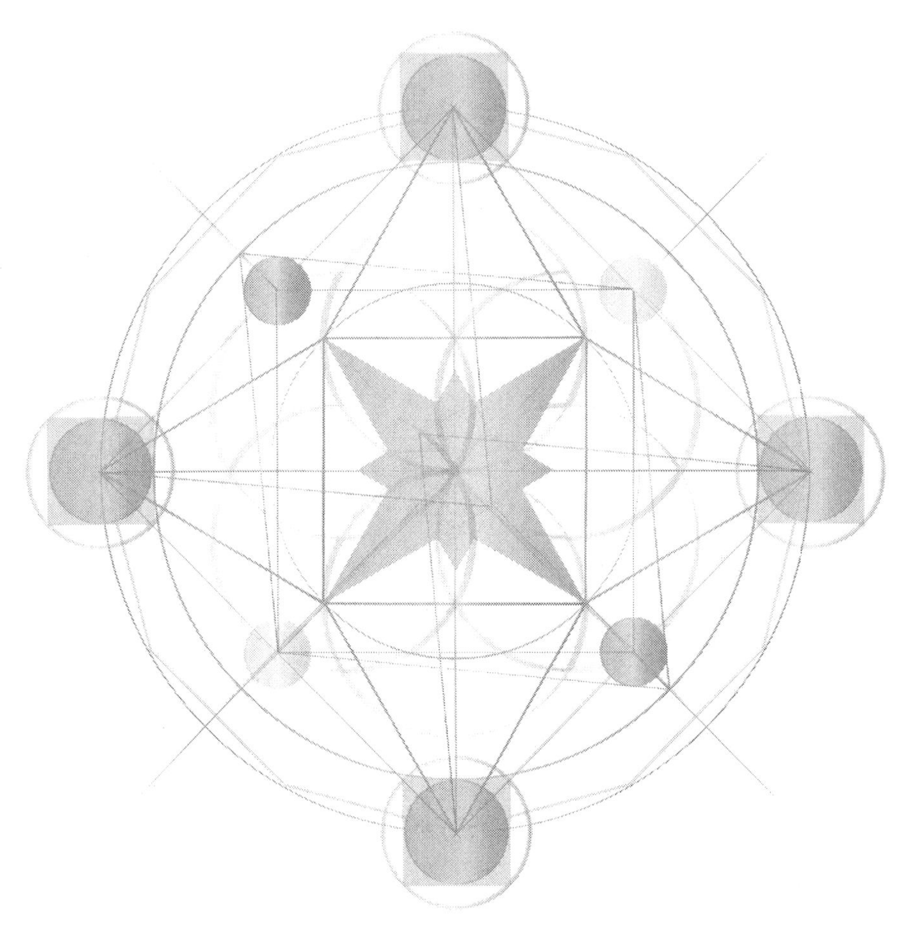

Making the Symbols Work

Once you have carefully read each agreement, set of guidelines, list of intentions, and supplemented them with specifications if you so choose, the information becomes integrated within you. You may not be able to consciously recall every detail on demand but it is impossible to un-know something after you have had exposure to the information. The specific details may be trapped in your memory archives, but you are forever connected in some capacity with that information.

As you are integrating the information in this book by reading it carefully, purposely create a connection among the directives outlined in each Agreement (to include your supplemental specifications), the corresponding symbol, associated affirmation, and personal goals:

Agreement > Symbol > Affirmation > Goals

	DIRECTIVE AGREEMENTS/ GUIDELINES INTENTIONS	SYMBOL	AFFIRMATION	ACTION	GOAL ACHIEVEMENT/ MANIFESTATION
ROLE OF THE CONSCIOUS MIND:	*delegate thoughts for planned outcomes*	*connect with visually*	*develop belief in goal achievement*	*what you "do" to achieve*	*expectation*
ROLE OF THE SUB-CONSCIOUS MIND:	*focus on delegated thoughts*	*reconnect with specifics of agreements, guidelines*	*reinforce beliefs in goal achievement*	*discern appropriate action based on beliefs*	*expectation*

You create this connection by first reading the Agreement in its entirety, then focusing on the visual of the symbol, saying the corresponding affirmation out loud, and finally stating your goal(s) with the intent to connect all elements.

After you have finished reading the directives/Agreements with optional supplements, stating your goal(s) and purposely associating those two things with their corresponding symbol and affirmation, you will be ready to delegate those Agreements, directives and particulars to your subconscious mind.

Repetition reinforces focus on the task—for example, doing a workout routine. Each time you look at the symbol associated with a particular set of directives and goals, and say the corresponding affirmation, you express your conscious desire to remain focused on that block of information. You also reinforce the belief that you will achieve your goal.

Using Symbols as a Daily Practice

Read the following Agreements, Guidelines and Intentions. Choose which ones apply to your life. Fill in the worksheet with any details or specifics you believe will enhance the value of the documents for you and state the goal you wish to achieve as a result. Keep your directives positive and focus on new outcomes with your articulation. Avoid rehashing dysfunction or calling attention to behavior you want to distance yourself from- in other words, don't dwell on what you don't want in your life.

For example: if you want to direct your subconscious to lead you away from emotional co-dependence in intimate relationships, use wording that supports emotional independence as a new outcome. Choose to use wording such as: "I expect to create emotional independence" rather than "I expect to stop engaging in emotional co-dependence."

There are blank spaces for you to fill to tailor each Agreement, set of Guidelines and Intentions documents to your specifications. There is also a blank space for you to state the associated goal you wish to achieve.

As you alter the documents and tailor them to convey specific focus and to relay your goals, connect the new versions with the accompanying symbols and affirmations. Remember, you do this by reading the new version of the document, focusing on the symbol for a few seconds and then saying the corresponding affirmation with the intention to link all of the components.

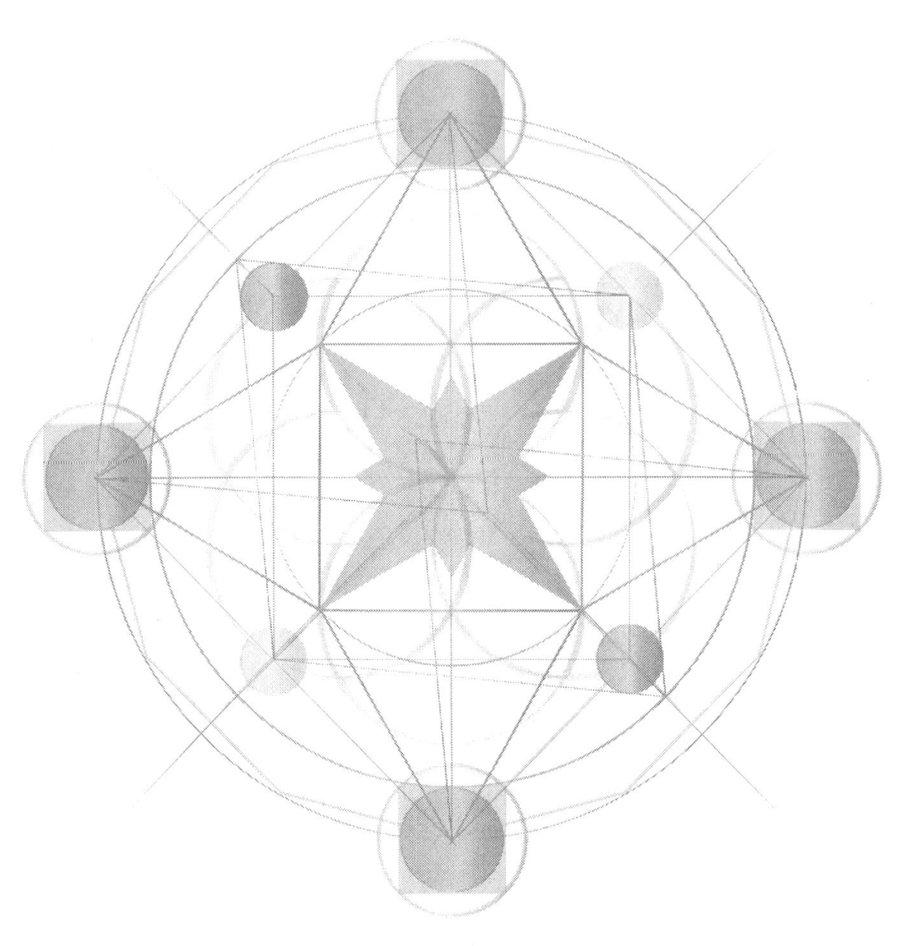

Grouping the Symbols

The symbols can be used individually to address specific issues or they can be used in clusters to build blueprints for significant life changes.

The symbols are broken down into three group themes:

GROUP 1: *Connecting with Your True Identity*

GROUP 2: *Searching the Higher Elements of Your Soul*

GROUP 3: *Expanding Your Reach Through Relationship*

The first group, **"Connecting with Your True Identity,"** facilitates the acknowledgement of who you truly are, helps you connect with your deep well of talents, and prepares you for making purposeful changes in your life.

As you go deeper into the process, the second group, **"Searching the Higher Elements of Your Soul,"** has you tap into the all-knowing part of yourself that shelters your archived soul memories. This group of directives enables you to harness the power to create your own environment in which to thrive. As you begin to unearth these higher elements of your soul and work with them, life feels more joyous and purposeful.

The third group, **"Expanding Your Reach Through Relationship,"** puts you in touch with the ability to generate connections and alignment on multiple personal and interpersonal levels. You re-build an un-inhibiting energetic infrastructure that allows you to exercise practical, efficient application of your talents by means of securing connectivity among the elements of your soul and connectivity between you and other members of the collective body of information with similar goals.

Group # 1

"Connecting with your True Identity"

"You're the result of the previous pictures you've painted for yourself... and you can always paint new ones."
—DR. WAYNE W. DYER

This grouping contains the following agreements, guidelines and intentions:

*Unveiling My True Self
*Improving My Life
*Connecting with Wisdom
*Preserving Earth
*Reserving Judgment
*Letting Go

The focus of this group is to clear away the clutter so that your true self is revealed to you. This is important because when you are distracted or overwhelmed by navigating life, you give your power away without even realizing it.

When you disconnect from your true self, your inner light slowly grows dim and it is easy to lose touch with your brilliance. This group of agreements, guidelines and intentions will provide a road map with the most direct route back to your authentic self.

© Intentional Healing Systems, LLC

Unveiling my True Self

"To say something nice about yourself, this is the hardest thing in the world for people to do. They'd rather take their clothes off."
—NANCY FRIDAY

We each have something unique and special to offer those we connect with and the world around us. Sometimes we unknowingly keep these things hidden from ourselves and others. The objective of the "Unveiling My True Self" Agreement is to allow what is extraordinary and wonderful about you to surface. As these talents and attributes are revealed, new doors and opportunities open in front of you.

You can use this agreement to help attract a romantic partner, secure a new job, attract better clients, improve friendships and family relationships, receive recognition for your accomplishments, and enhance your contribution to humanity.

You may find that as you commit your subconscious to the terms of this agreement that people view you as changed and react to you differently. Make note of any welcomed reactions and re-focus on creating more of those reactions in the future.

1. Unveiling my True self

I, ____________________, agree to…

1. …always remember that my true self is drawn out by giving love and receiving love.
2. …allow others to see the brightest part of my light.
3. …choose light and love over dark and fear whenever there is opportunity.
4. …stay centered in truth at all times.
5. …feed the heart of my soul by doing things I love.
6. …seek the company of others who emanate the light of their sacred hearts.
7. …make time to share with people who balance the exchange of love with me.
8. …be as generous as possible by sharing my resources without sacrificing my well-being.
9. …be kind to all living beings.
10. …make efforts to inspire others to be kind to one another.
11. …operate from a place of high integrity at all times.
12. …let my light illuminate the pathway of my journey.

Personalizing the Agreement to Unveil Your True Self:

"I am emanating light"

Additional directives to create focus:

Suggested goals: name people and types of people you wish to attract attentions from or inspire, to showcase your uniqueness or to overcome insecurities.

Your goal to achieve in association with this agreement:

© Intentional Healing Systems, LLC

Improving my Life

It is a soul urge to improve oneself. That is what life is about, constant and never-ending improvement, whether it is a conscious goal or something that prods from the shadows. With each new day, we take a step forward on our journey and our soul sets out to be better than we were the day before.

The objective of the "Improving My Life" Agreement is to create parameters that only allow for attention to be given to situations, events, opportunities and relationships that change your life in new ways that honor you. The guidelines provide additional safeguards that protect you from falling back into patterns that no longer serve you. For example, you may think that you always have to "learn the hard way," but at a certain point, that belief holds you back.

You can use this agreement to inspire changes that greatly improve the quality of your life such as attracting a loving partner, making friends after moving to a new location, advancing your career with a new job or a better position, and making a new start in life.

2. Improving my Life

I, ____________________, expect to…

1. …create favorable outcomes within my power.
2. …attract people into my life who honor my highest good.
3. …treat myself and all others with respect.
4. …develop relationships that inspire me to offer the best of myself
5. …operate from the highest ground possible in all situations.
6. …clearly envision what I intend to create in my life.
7. …seize opportunities to make life easier and more interesting.
8. …remember that I am worthy of what I wish for.
9. …allow support from those who offer.
10. …adjust my goals to honor my highest good.
11. …draw creative and financial resources toward me with ease to meet my needs
12. …allow grace and ease to be the standard that diverts me from chaos and distraction

Personalizing the Guidelines to Improve Your Life:

"I am improving my life"

Additional directives to create focus:

Suggested goals: name people, types of people, scenarios (such as jobs, social situations or personal circumstances) you wish to attract or inspire.

Your goal to achieve in association with these guidelines:

Connecting with Wisdom

"Action in the world, and reflection on it, go hand in hand."

"Where do you start when reflecting on your experience? Let's make it simple. You can start with this question: Who do I want to be?"

—Eric Greitens, Resilience

The simple truth is that we naturally cultivate wisdom through the act of living. So regardless of whether or not you have a formal education, have traveled the world or stayed put in your own backyard, dined with dignitaries or gone hungry, you have effectively developed your own brand of wisdom. Your wisdom has the power to bring you to the next set of crossroads in each moment of your life journey.

It is easy to take your own wisdom for granted because it is so familiar to you, so it doesn't necessarily seem special. We have a tendency to dismiss information we consider to be of no real value and bury it in our archives. However, your buried wisdom is special and can be of great use to you when you choose to connect with it.

The intentions laid out in this "Connecting with Wisdom" Agreement pay homage to you and the treasure trove of wisdom you have spent your entire life amassing. You can use these intentions to refine and enhance your skills, to be a role model to others and to master your communication skills.

3. *Connecting with Wisdom*

I, ____________________, intend to…

1. …draw on all of the lessons of my life to guide me now.
2. …be open to the wisdom shared by others.
3. …easily recall details of past experiences that can assist me now.
4. …form a secured connection with the all-knowing higher part of me, my Higher Wisdom.
5. …draw on the collective experiences of groups and individuals I choose to associate with or emulate.
6. …contemplate actions before I engage in them.
7. …make decisions based on thoughts rather than impulses.
8. …use discernment in all situations.
9. …capitalize on my strengths.
10. ...trust my intuition.
11. …follow my truth.
12. …put my knowledge to work.

Personalizing the Intentions to Connect with Wisdom:

"I am wise"

Additional directives to create focus:

____

____

____

____

____

____

____

____

Suggested goals: to put more trust in yourself when making decisions, to build self-confidence for a specific event, communicate better with others (specify names), refine a specific skill, improve your memory.

Your goal to achieve in association with these intentions:

____

____

____

____

____

____

____

© Intentional Healing Systems, LLC

Preserving Earth

"We do not inherit the world from our ancestors.
We borrow it from our children."
—Author Unknown

Most of us are aware of the changes our Mother Earth is experiencing and it has become of prime importance for each of us to participate in the preservation of this planet we call home. Each day the media tells us the true stories of natural disasters and man-made disasters that literally change the landscape of Earth. We have little to no control over destruction caused by natural disasters, but we have absolute control over the destruction caused by mankind. We just have to put Earth's preservation at the top of our to-do list if we truly want to create favorable change.

While we have come a long way in the past few decades with preservation practices, we still have room for improvement. Human beings in many parts of the world have become accustomed to modern conveniences, and economies are driven by consumption and exchange of currency. Conveniences and consumption often translate to waste.

Even if a person has no intentions to pollute and makes what he considers to be reasonable efforts to practice conservation and preservation, there may be more he can do to preserve Earth if he tasks his subconscious to prompt him to act.

You can use the “Preserving Earth” Agreement to spark remembrance of checking for recycling stamps before you throw a container away, to turn off the water while you are brushing your teeth, sharing your knowledge of going green and conservation with others, minimizing use of chemicals, and increasing your awareness regarding preservation practices of establishments you patronize.

4. Preserving Earth

"I am committed to Mother Earth"

I, ______________________, agree to…

1. …do my best to preserve nature.
2. …use natural resources sparingly.
3. …be thoughtful about my disposal practices.
4. …reduce my carbon footprint.
5. …reuse and recycle as much as possible.
6. …avoid the use of harmful chemicals unless it is absolutely necessary.
7. …respect and recognize the gifts offered by all living beings.
8. …protect animals when at all possible.
9. …promote the growth of plants in appropriate places.
10. …notice and appreciate the beauty of nature.
11. …connect with the vibration of Earth by spending time outdoors.
12. …support companies that actively engage in sustainability practices.

Personalizing the Agreement to Preserve Mother Earth:

"I am committed to Mother Earth"

Additional directives to create focus:

____

____

____

____

____

____

____

____

Suggested goals: to identify and recycle all recyclables, research sustainability practices of companies who make your favorite products, increase efforts to conserve water and take every opportunity to inspire others to conserve.

Your goal to achieve in association with this agreement:

____

____

____

____

____

____

Reserving Judgment

"The question is not what you look at--but what you see."
—Henry David Thoreau

"Releasing judgment of another is actually releasing judgment of yourself."
—Dr. Wayne W. Dyer

It is a function of human nature to judge but can often be destructive in the context of personal and professional relationships. Unreserved judgment can also keep us trapped in certain mindsets that aren't necessarily based in truth.

It is important to know how and when to use judgment to your advantage. When you use judgment to honor your well-being and the well-being of others, it is called "discernment". There is a thought process behind discernment that makes it much more refined than unchecked judgment. Discernment is logical and thoughtful, while unreserved judgment is impulsive and invites discord.

When you are in the middle of an emotional situation or you don't have the luxury of time to contemplate your immediate judgments, it can be difficult to rein in your feelings and reserve judgment in favor of exercising discernment. The "Reserving Judgment" Agreement can help inspire you to naturally reserve judgment and remain emotionally neutral until you can call on your intellect to examine the circumstances or another person's motives.

Once you have taken your time and considered the situation and/or person from different perspectives, your judgments will become more meaningful with greater potential to produce benevolent outcomes. Sometimes discernment yields the same results as judgments, but your views of the situation or person become expanded and you gain growth from that.

This agreement can help you to create harmony in personal or professional relationships you have struggled with, to gain exposure to new ideas, to inspire you to be more tolerant of others, to promote peace, and to appreciate differences you may have feared at another time in your life.

5. Reserving Judgment

"I am exercising a new perspective"

I, ____________________, agree to…

1. …engage in the practice of reserving judgment over making impulse assumptions
2. …take inventory of the good qualities in others before noticing any other attributes
3. …celebrate the differences in people
4. …celebrate the similarities in people
5. …allow others the right to their opinions
6. …exercise confidence in new situations
7. …try new things
8. …put myself in others shoes
9. …use intellectual discernment over emotional judgment
10. …choose to connect with kind thoughts and push all other thoughts away
11. …make every effort to bring out the best in others with my thoughts and actions
12. …remember that everything happens for a reason

Personalizing the Agreement to Reserve Judgment:

"I am exercising a new perspective"

Additional directives to create focus:

Suggested goals: name people you would like to get along with, inspire peaceful exchanges during specific events, or ease your fears.

Your goal(s) to achieve in association with this agreement:

© Intentional Healing Systems, LLC

Letting Go

"Sometimes you wake up. Sometimes the fall kills you. And sometimes, when you fall, you fly."
—Neil Gaiman, Sandman

Many of us struggle with behavior patterns that cause us harm and keep us stuck in uncomfortable situations. Often the reason we cycle with these patterns is because subconsciously we dwell on the dysfunction. Our underlying focus influences what we create for ourselves and if we are perpetually focused on destructive behavior, then we create outcomes in alignment with destructive energies. We focus on what we don't want and therefore we get more of it!

We are constantly creating. Energy continues to move and with each breath we take, we are given the opportunity to create something new—or old. It is our choice what we create next. We can choose to stay stuck by continuing to hold on to old patterns that prompt us to create what no longer honors us, or we can move forward and let go of old patterns, circumstances and behaviors.

This agreement can be used to break the chain of destructive and/or old patterns by shifting underlying focus. As we program our subconscious to shift focus to our limitless potential, we begin to connect with the inspiration that supports us in our endeavors to create new behaviors, situations and relationships that replace the old.

6. *Letting Go*

"I am releasing the past"

I, ____________________, agree to…

1. …forgive myself for my perceived failures
2. …forgive others for their transgressions
3. …retain the lessons from all of my experiences
4. …release the pains resulting from my experiences
5. …appreciate the growth inspired by my experiences
6. …let the past remain in the past
7. …bring new energy forward
8. …focus my attention on the here and now
9. …allow myself to evolve into someone new and improved
10. …release the idea that I am bound by previous limitations
11. …change my mind when it feels right
12. …believe that breaking a cycle is a choice I am able to exercise

Personalizing the Agreement to Let Go:

"I am releasing the past"

Additional directives to create focus:

____

____

____

____

____

____

____

____

Suggested goals: forming productive habits that replace destructive ones, forgiveness of yourself, forgiveness of others (name them) and inviting new experiences that honor your highest good.

Your goal to achieve in association with this agreement:

____

____

____

____

____

____

____

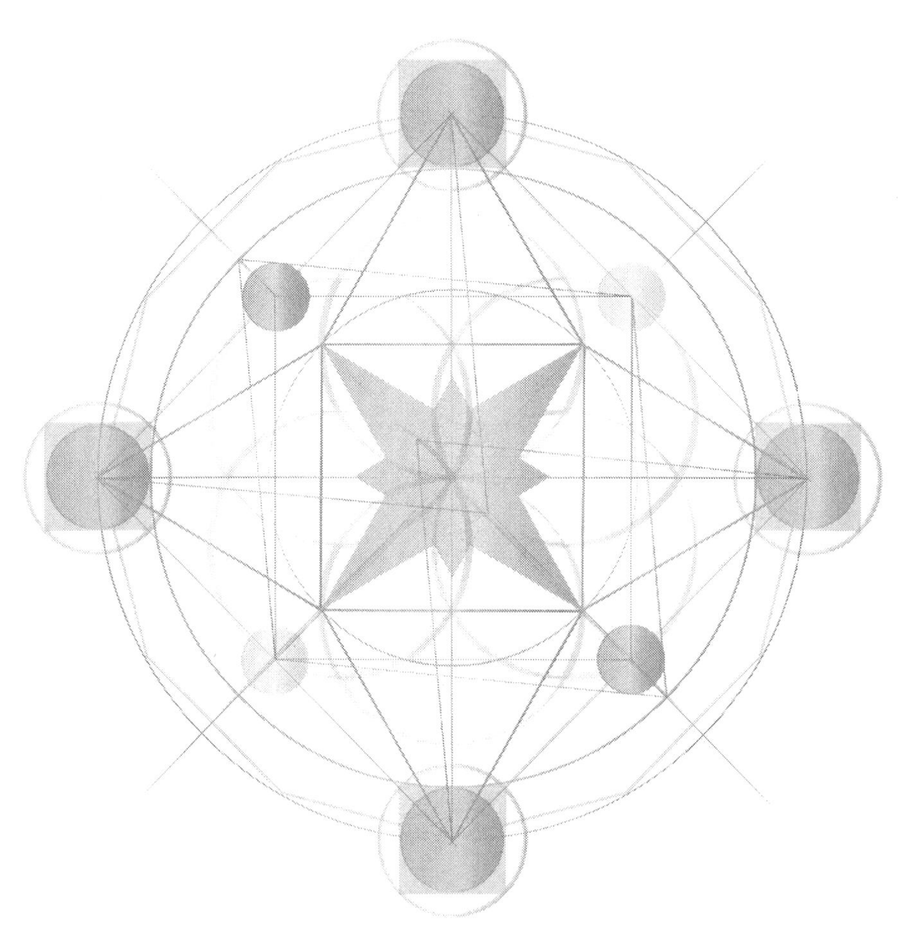

Group # 2

"Searching the Higher Elements of Your Soul"

"We delight in the beauty of the butterfly, but rarely admit the changes it has gone through to achieve that beauty."
—*Maya Angelou*

This grouping contains the following Agreements, Guidelines and Intentions:

*Expressing Gratitude
*Appreciating Myself
*Creating Filters
*Clearing my Space
*Manifesting Visions
*Expanding Awareness

The directives outlined in this group set your subconscious to focus on unearthing your innate talents and abilities. As you bring these gems to the surface, you gain easy access to their magic. You can choose to use these tools, at will, for the greater good of yourself and others. The result of putting these talents to work is exponential accelerated growth and the rich, expanded depth of your consciousness.

© Intentional Healing Systems, LLC

Expressing Gratitude

"Be thankful for what you have. You'll end up having more... The single greatest thing you can do to change your life today would be to start being grateful for what you have right now."
—Oprah Winfrey

Life itself is a gift. It can be difficult to remember this when you are feeling tested or weary, but the most primal parts of us are programmed to fight for life regardless of personal circumstances. Therefore, it is something to value, and most would be hard pressed to argue against this point.

There is a direct relationship between the degree of gratitude a person connects with and expresses and a person's level of emotional, mental and spiritual development. The more a person integrates the concept and use of gratitude in their daily practice, the more evolved they are. A person that has the genuine ability to feel grateful for each and every thing they experience, whether he or she (or society) considers those things to be good or bad, is a highly conscious, evolved being.

We are here, experiencing multiple incarnations, to ultimately master being human by way of expanding our consciousness. On the grand scale, the Gratitude Agreement can help set you on a course that facilitates development of this important mastery skill.

A more specific use of this agreement could include creating more comfort in your life, creating solidarity with others, taking responsibility for your choices, and easing the pain from emotional and mental trauma.

7. Expressing Gratitude

"I am grateful for my experiences"

I, ______________________, agree to…

1. …identify a benefit in every experience
2. …integrate the underlying lessons of all situations I participate in
3. …view all experiences as learning opportunities
4. …value each exchange with another person as a gift of growth
5. …recognize that I am a collective product of my experiences
6. …celebrate the wisdom I have cultivated
7. …recognize and appreciate the roles of others in my development
8. …remember that overcoming painful situations allows for profound expansion
9. …genuinely appreciate all of the good things in my life
10. …remember that outcomes are based on the choices I make
11. …honor myself with the understanding that I am here to learn and grow my soul
12. …remember that my expansion benefits collective human evolution

Personalizing the Agreement to Express Gratitude:

"I am grateful for my experiences"

Additional directives to create focus:

____

____

____

____

____

____

____

____

Suggested goals: finding value in painful situations, identifying value in specific relationships, taking responsibility for your choices, looking at situations from different perspectives and reducing pressure you put on yourself.

Your goal to achieve in association with this agreement:

____

____

____

____

____

____

© Intentional Healing Systems, LLC

Appreciating Myself

"You, yourself, as much as anybody in the entire universe, deserve your love and affection."
—BUDDHA

We are our own worst critics. Most of us judge and criticize ourselves freely in our subconscious thoughts without censorship. Furthermore, we are taught to associate egotism with self-appreciation, but the two concepts sit at opposite ends of the spectrum.

The difference is that genuine, honest self-appreciation is creatively constructive while fear-based egotism, which sits on a foundation of illusions, can be a destructive force.

Earnest self-appreciation is the basis for appreciation of others as well. When a person recognizes herself as worthy, she gains the ability to fill any voids in her heart with self-love. She becomes whole and never feels as if she desperately needs the help or validation of another person to give her something she feels she is missing.

We achieve emotional independence through self-appreciation, which is not to say that we lose the desire to have relationships. Emotional independence gives us the freedom to view giving and receiving love from others as a choice. It also recalibrates our expectations of others. We allow ourselves to let others give to us what comes naturally for them rather than having expectations that they will fill voids based on our needs. We begin to appreciate others for who they are and not for whom we want or expect them to be.

This agreement can be used to help establish emotional independence, build self-respect, gain confidence, and attract healthy relationships or life conditions.

8. Appreciating Myself

I, ____________________, agree to…

1. …recognize my unique gifts
2. …remember that I am a valuable contributor to collective humanity
3. …view myself as equal to any and all other human beings
4. …accept that I was created for a purpose of great value
5. …appreciate myself
6. …allow others to love me
7. …give myself permission to love who I am in this moment
8. …remember that self-love can never be revoked by anyone else
9. …be proud of who I have become
10. …stay focused on love
11. …love myself without conditions
12. …believe that I am worthy of love

Personalizing the Agreement to Appreciate Yourself:

"I am worthy"

Additional directives to create focus:

____

____

____

____

____

____

____

____

____

Suggested goals: gain confidence, feel more worthy, feel "whole", promote or attract healthy personal and professional relationships.

Your goal to achieve in association with this agreement:

____

____

____

____

____

____

____

© Intentional Healing Systems, LLC

Creating Filters

"If we see a sad rain, it doesn't mean the rain is sad, but it means we see it. That's an easily dismissible kind of projection. But what I'm struggling to say, is that we take that rain in through our own hearts and emotions and senses and skin, and all those filters have an impact."

—*Karen Joy Fowler*

Generally speaking, as a conscious person, one can choose to create parameters for her journey that disallow the birth and growth of fear. These parameters create a general sense of safety and confidence in the subconscious, which effectively negates unreasonable fear.

Caution is always appropriate, especially with regards to safety issues but many of us give unfounded fear the power to paralyze us and often we make decisions based on it. These decisions may inhibit enjoyment and prevent us from participating in life.

Filters are more constructive and allow us to create a channel for receiving and integrating energy we identify as favorable. Filters also help repel and divert unfavorable energies, reducing the likelihood that they will influence us subconsciously. This calming of subconscious turmoil helps us to enjoy greater levels of underlying peace and comfort, and affords us more opportunities to live life to the fullest extent.

This agreement can be used to help reduce worry or self-doubt, promote feeling emotionally and mentally "present", and increase enjoyment in life.

9. *Creating Filters*

I, ____________________, expect to…

1. …request and receive the protection of my Guides, Angels and Masters to insulate me
2. …feel the connection with my Higher Wisdom at all times
3. …ground myself and allow Mother Earth to stabilize me
4. …neutralize my fears by calling on thoughts based in love
5. …only allow experiences that speak to my highest good to affect me
6. …only absorb surrounding energies that brighten the emanations of my inner light
7. …take deep breaths to calm myself when I feel uncomfortable
8. …surround myself with the golden light emanations of my sacred heart
9. …remember that my Higher Wisdom will only give me experiences I am equipped to handle
10. …use my sensitivities to heighten awareness in situations where I feel unsafe
11. …feel emotionally and physically protected
12. …live in each moment as it unfolds

Personalizing the Guidelines to Create Filters:

"I am safe"

Additional directives to create focus:

____

Suggested goals: do more things (or something specific) that you enjoy, increase feelings of security, experience peace of mind and create more comfort in life.

Your goal to achieve in association with these guidelines:

Clearing my Space

"There is no gate, no lock, no bolt that you can set upon the freedom of my mind."
—Virginia Woolf

We identify ourselves as being part of a "whole" on the soul level, so many of us crave companionship and are drawn to connecting with others. Sometimes connection comes at a price because we inadvertently take on the unfavorable energy of others as we get close.

Science has confirmed we are empathic by nature. Even if you do not identify this quality in yourself, it is present to a degree, which means you feel some part of what others around you feel. Some of us are better at letting the energy of others go, but if you are not one of those people, it is important to maintain the integrity of your personal space by clearing the build-up of collected energy away.

It is also helpful to set up some guidelines that dictate which energies are permitted to enter and fortify your field going forward. This will take nothing away from your interactions with others but it will allow you to experience greater clarity and block energies that do not serve you.

This set of guidelines can be helpful to those who work in public places or those who interact with volumes of people as a function of their profession. These guidelines can also assist with creating clarity for the purposes of healing or regenerating the physical body.

10. Clearing my Space

I, ____________________, expect to…

1. …secure my personal space by creating a golden bubble around me
2. …push all of the existing energy that no longer honors me out of the bubble until it glows with golden light
3. …secure the room or space I am in by enclosing it within a golden bubble
4. …push all of the existing energy that no longer honors me and the people who surround me out of the bubble until it glows with golden light
5. …invite the golden energy stored in my sacred heart to be released through my body so each and every cell is bathed in golden, healing light
6. …hydrate my body adequately with water
7. …be drawn toward eating whole foods that nourish and repair my cells
8. …repel and block implementation of toxic emotional energies by exuding love
9. …use my physical systems to filter out and neutralize physical toxins to the best of my ability
10. …feel compelled to take deep breaths to circulate regenerative energy most efficiently
11. …feel drawn to places and situations that honor my highest and best good
12. …feel compelled to connect with Mother Nature and allow her to help me clear my space.

Personalizing the Guidelines to Clear Your Space:

"I am clear"

Additional directives to create focus:

____

____

____

____

____

____

____

____

Suggested goals: create prime energy conditions for physical and emotional healing, cleanse personal space after working closely with others.

Your goal to achieve in association with these guidelines:

____

____

____

____

____

____

____

© Intentional Healing Systems, LLC

Manifesting Visions

"Life isn't about finding yourself. Life is about creating yourself."
—George Bernard Shaw

We are creators. Some people have artfully mastered this process while others are still in training. We all have great potential in this arena, but like anything, it requires planning, dedication and focus to be skilled at creating. Creation begins with goal setting. Once you have identified your goal, you then create a vision of what that manifested goal looks like. Your actions aligned with your goal lead you down a guided pathway from the goal to your manifested vision. These three elements combined (goal, vision and actions) are a basic recipe for willful creation. Support for willful creation comes from our underlying focus that is the responsibility of our subconscious mind.

That said, we often create haphazardly in a collage since few of us begin the creation process by delegating thoughts to our subconscious mind. When we set goals, regardless of whether we envision the ideal manifestation and engage in supportive actions, we often unknowingly allow our subconscious to do the heavy lifting without direction. Then we are disappointed when we don't achieve what we plan to.

This set of intentions in the Manifesting Visions Agreement can help you to purposely manage the part of the creation process that is supported by subconscious activity. These intentions are general and aim to train your subconscious to automatically provide an energetic atmosphere conducive to creating. The conscious part of the creation process, which includes identifying a goal, creating a vision of your manifested goal, and then choosing to partake in actions that align with that vision, requires active participation. Your subconscious will help guide and support you in your achievement with use of these intentions.

11. *Manifesting Visions*

"I am creating new outcomes"

I, ____________________, intend to…

1. …only participate in situations that honor my highest and best good
2. …use each new day to exercise what I learned the previous day
3. …view the events of the day as I would like them to play out
4. …only accept energies that promote my higher level objectives
5. …move forward in my soul development
6. …accept my role as a creator
7. …believe I have the ability to shape my journey
8. …use love to fuel and accelerate new outcomes
9. …choose pathways that allow me to create without resistance
10. …identify and dismantle potential obstacles
11. …always have the expectation that all will be well
12. …manage my thoughts, words, emotions and actions to support my expected outcomes

Personalizing the Intentions to Manifest Visions:

"I am creating new outcomes"

Additional directives to create focus:

Suggested goals: improve the quality of your life, recover from something, rebuild your life, create financial security and realize a dream, use your skills in new and more productive ways.

Your goal to achieve in association with these intentions:

© Intentional Healing Systems, LLC

Expanding Awareness

"What we are now seeing is a world that is connected."
—John Chambers, Cisco Systems

An expanded level of awareness can bring with it a host of valuable gifts such as more knowledge, deeper understanding of events and relationships, the ability to view situations from multiple perspectives, connectivity with other human beings and profound compassion for others, to name a few. Increased awareness, as with wisdom, is a natural and welcomed development throughout the course of life.

There is no set timetable or rate at which a person expands her awareness. The evolution depends on the journey a person chooses to take, but effort and a will to reach heightened levels of consciousness can greatly impact the development of it.

This set of guidelines in the Expanding Awareness Agreement helps to direct you toward experiencing new depths of consciousness by reinforcing your desire to connect with the foundational elements that build higher, more benevolent levels of existence.

12. Expanding Awareness

I, ____________________, expect to…

1. … view each exchange with another person as an opportunity to learn something new
2. … unveil more of my innate gifts
3. …bring light to a situation or relationship I did not previously understand
4. …always connect with the highest form of truth in any situation
5. …use and trust my intuition to guide me
6. …see situations from the perspective of others as well as from my own
7. …keep an open line of connection with my Higher Wisdom at all times
8. …connect with people who offer unique points of view
9. …have exposure to experiences that shift my perceptions
10. …find interest in new ideas and concepts
11. …keep my mind open
12. …call forward any archived soul memories that serve me now

Personalizing the Guidelines to Expand Awareness:

"I am fully aware"

Additional directives to create focus:

____

____

____

____

____

____

____

____

Suggested goals: connect more deeply with others, exude compassion, increase understanding of what has been gained from life events and heighten intuition.

Your goal to achieve in association with these guidelines:

____

____

____

____

____

____

____

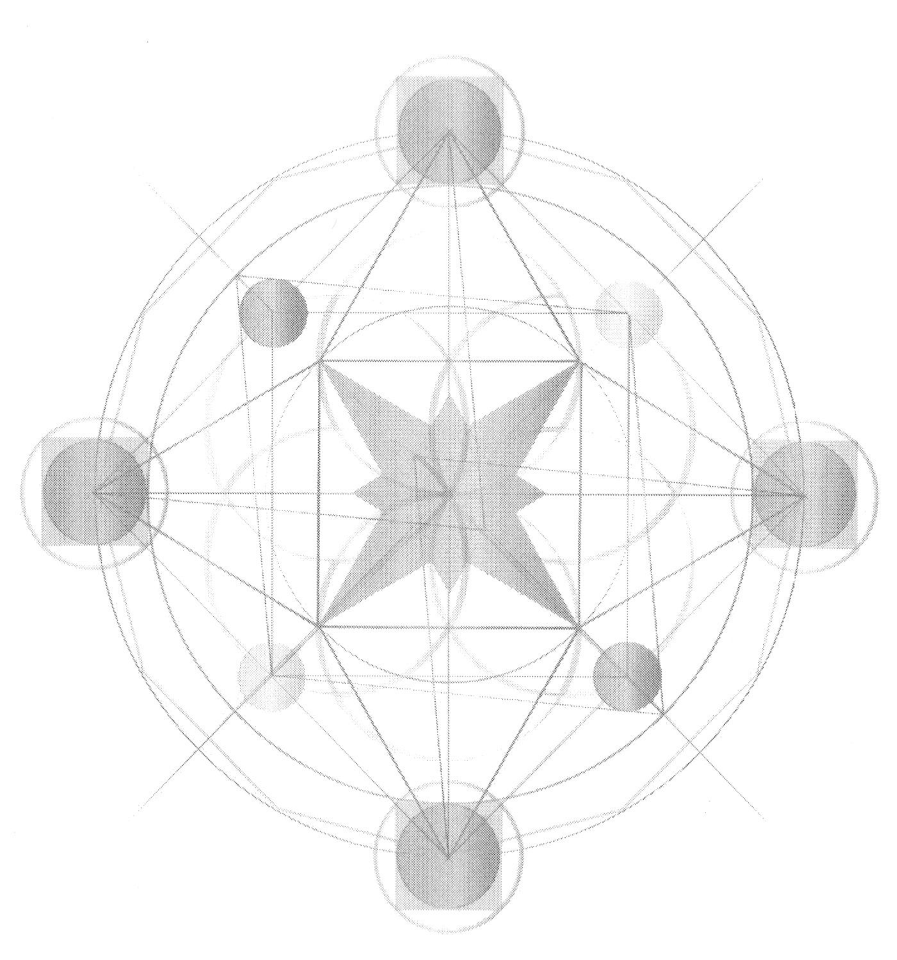

Group # 3

"Expanding your Reach through Relationship"

"It is good to love many things, for therein lies the true strength, and whosoever loves much performs much, and can accomplish much, and what is done in love is well done."
—*Vincent Van Gogh*

This grouping contains the following Agreements, Guidelines and Intentions:

*Activating Knowledge
*Promoting Unity
*Having a Good Day
*Optimizing Digestion
*Exercising Personal Power
*Instituting Joy

Connectivity, relationship or alignment must be present for movement to occur in an efficient and effective manner. If you want to alter something about yourself, you must examine the connections between your beliefs and thoughts, your thoughts and emotions, and/or your emotions and actions to make a viable plan for change:

Beliefs and Thoughts > Thoughts and Emotions > Emotions and Actions

If you want to create change in your community, you must consort with others and work together to make change happen in a successful way. The agreements, guidelines and intentions in this grouping help you to create connectivity, alignment and relationship within yourself for personal development, as well as to pair your innate talents with other like-minded people to affect global change for the greater good of all humanity.

© Intentional Healing Systems, LLC

Activating Knowledge

"Knowledge is love and light and vision."
—*Helen Keller*

The knowledge we accumulate carries immeasurable power through the potential harnessed in what we do with it. Knowledge itself though, holds little value until it is applied in some way (through imagination). The application of knowledge comes in many forms. We could choose to work in a specific field to make use of our knowledge. We could apply our knowledge to doing things we enjoy. We could use our knowledge to teach others. The possibilities are without limits.

We often have preconceived notions about how to apply knowledge. Sometimes we even believe that the knowledge we possess has no worth. If you learned a particular trade or pursued a degree that doesn't correspond with what you do to make a living, it doesn't mean that what you learned is rendered useless or was a waste of your time. It only means that you may have to exercise some creativity (and imagination) to apply it.

Some of us feel compelled to actively contribute our knowledge to collective humanity, but whether you feel driven to do so is irrelevant. We each contribute to the collective whole by virtue of the fact that we are part of the collective. Whatever we do to apply our knowledge in a productive way indirectly affects everyone living on this planet.

This set of intentions can be used to remind yourself of how valuable the application of your knowledge can be. It is meant to inspire you to take every opportunity to better yourself using what you know in creative ways and to actively contribute to the collective humanity.

13. Activating Knowledge

"I am activating my knowledge"

I, ____________________, intend to…

1. …be a role model to others
2. …teach something to another person today
3. …keep my memory clear and sharp
4. …remember whatever knowledge I have gathered that will assist me today
5. …use what I know to make the world a better place
6. …always exercise my ingenuity
7. …produce creative solutions to obstacles that hinder me
8. …weigh my options and make thoughtful choices
9. …trust what I know to be truth
10. …use the skills I have developed
11. …seek opportunities to supplement and enhance my knowledge
12. …cultivate wisdom with the knowledge I have amassed

Personalizing the Intentions to Activate Knowledge:

"I am activating my knowledge"

Additional directives to create focus:

Suggested goals: Use your skills in new and more productive ways, boost your creativity and find new ways to share what you know.

Your goal to achieve in association with these intentions:

TM

Promoting Unity

"To become a true global citizen, one must abandon all notions of 'otherness' and instead embrace 'togetherness'."
—*Suzy Kassem*

Unity is the heart of peace. There can be no peace without Unity and there can be no Unity without U and I. As we prepare to step across the threshold of what has been termed "The Golden Age of Peace," we must integrate, promote and revere Unity as an irrevocable standard.

We live in an era where we can procure information effortlessly. It sits at the end of our fingertips. Digital pictures and videos displaying atrocities of war being fought on the other side of the world, the ravages of natural disasters and human suffering in poor nations can sweep across our computer screens instantaneously. There are no longer boundaries of time and space between human beings.

Technology has evolved in a way that makes it easy for us to perceive how connected every human being is to one another. Technological progression has planted the seeds of Unity and it is up to us to nurture the growth.

While we have been bombarded with images of the hardships of humanity it can't be lost on us that bearing witness to such pain ignites compassion in our hearts and fuels a desire to draw closer together.

Taking even small measures to act on behalf of our compassion is what will change this world forever.

This Unity Agreement serves as a sacred oath and demonstrates your commitment to promoting Unity for the benefit of all mankind.

14. Promoting Unity

"I am One, and One for All."

I ____________________, agree to:

1. …Believe and acknowledge that we are all created equal by forces greater than any individual.
2. …View each human being as an extension of myself because we, as individuals, create the "all", together.
3. …Recognize and appreciate the very best qualities in myself and others before I allow myself to make any other judgments.
4. …Be kind to myself and others.
5. …Express gratitude for the learning potential in each exchange I have with another.
6. …Forgive myself and others for perceived imperfections.
7. …Celebrate the uniqueness and differences of each individual I share this beautiful planet with.
8. …Make every effort to improve this world for myself and all of mankind.
9. …Teach children, through my example, to love above all else.
10. …Create abundant opportunities to promote harmony, peace and unity with grace, compassion and love from the depths of my sacred heart.
11. …Preserve Mother Earth through thoughtful use of resources and disposal practices.
12. …Shine the light of my soul through my thoughts, words and actions.

Personalizing the Agreement to Promote Unity:

"I am One, and One for All."

Additional directives to create focus:

Suggested goals: contributing to new levels of peace, seizing opportunities to bring people together, and teaching your children how to improve the world.

Your goal to achieve in association with this agreement:

© Intentional Healing Systems, LLC

Having a Good Day

"The breeze at dawn has secrets to tell you. / Don't go back to sleep."

—RUMI

Each of your days can reflect the sacred being of light that you are. Beginning each day with the intention that it is going to be a good one has the power to influence emotions you produce in reaction to actual events as they unfold. You are more likely to actually experience what you consider to be a good day if you are in a mind-set that accepts it as a given, and even a right.

Your perception dictates what is real to you. Even if you are having a terrible day by someone else's standards, if your mind is conditioned to believe that your day is good, then what you experience still weighs in as good to you. You are less affected by the so-called bad and you may not even respond to it because it simply doesn't register.

This just shows you that we are equipped with the ability to steer our emotions with our thoughts. If we use our thoughts to inspire emotional reactions, we get to choose how we feel about anything that happens to us, including the events and exchanges of any given day. Our emotional reactions over the course of the day act as our rating scale for the day itself. If we are happy for a greater part of the day than it is generally a good day.

The intentions in the Good Day Agreement are meant to help you invite what you perceive to be good into your field on a daily basis.

15. Having a Good Day

I, ____________________, intend to…

1. …believe I am always connected with the all-knowing, higher part of myself.
2. …allow my higher self to guide me through the day with grace and ease.
3. …clear my energy field of thoughts and emotions that dim my light
4. …keep the area around me clear throughout my day by staying focused on love
5. …receive and integrate only the highest form of truth, the purest form of love and only the energies that honor my highest and best good today and always.
6. …reject all energies outside the parameters of the description in directive #5.
7. …emanate the light and love of my pure sacred heart as a gift to others I connect with on my journey today.
8. …support and promote the success of myself and others for purposes of creating a better world.
9. …be guided toward healthy habits and harmonious exchanges for the duration of the day.
10. …experience a heightened sense of awareness to gain new insights and enrich my soul with grace and ease today and always.

11. …connect with soul remembrance of my unique talents and skills to exercise creativity and do my part to better the world today and always.
12. …seal my energy field with love so that only the energies serving my highest and best good permeate the layers of my field in a balanced, harmonious and graceful way.

Personalizing the Intentions to Have a Good Day:

"I am sacred"

Additional directives to create focus:

____

____

____

____

____

____

____

Suggested goals: appreciate each day, find more value in what occupies your time and get more enjoyment from your work.

Your goal to achieve in association with these intentions:

____

____

____

____

© Intentional Healing Systems, LLC

Optimizing Digestion

"One cannot think well, love well, sleep well, if one has not dined well."
—*Virginia Woolf*

Eating sits at the top of the list of things a person does completely on purpose. It is hard to argue that you engage in the act of eating without conscious knowledge of what you are doing. Eating also happens to be one of the things that people struggle desperately with. So many of us are caught in the battle between placating our emotions with food and sustaining our bodies with sensible eating habits.

When we succumb to the urges of eating for purposes other than sustainment, we run the risk of making bad choices. Then when we feel terrible about ourselves and regret sits in the pit of our personal power center. No part of this scenario is productive.

This list of intentions in the Optimizing Digestion Agreement serves a similar purpose as the cross-cultural practice of saying grace or a blessing at mealtimes, in that the agreement raises your level of awareness about the sustainment of life with food. The intentions speak to your subconscious and help inspire you to make conscious, purposeful choices about eating. It gently reminds you through subconscious focus that eating is a way to honor and rejuvenate your body, and that your body is a precious gift to your spirit. These intentions also give the directive to infuse your digestion process with loving energies present in your energy field, so that in the event you choose to indulge, then you won't feel inclined to beat yourself up over the setback.

16. Optimizing digestion

"I am implementing only what honors me"

I, ______________________, expect to…

1. …Only produce cravings for foods that balance, remedy, nourish and hydrate me.
2. …Use energy to surround my whole digestive track with light to promote optimal absorption of nutrients.
3. …Use the energy of love to purify the food and drink I am about to consume.
4. …Instruct my body to metabolize food in the most efficient and effective manner
5. …Allow the beneficial nutrients of food to circulate to all parts of my body.
6. …Allow the regenerative and healing qualities of my food to fully integrate with all parts of my body.
7. …Allow myself to fully enjoy what I choose to eat
8. …Allow for all changes to my body associated with this meal to be implemented with grace and ease.
9. …Only integrate the energies of this meal that promote wellness and speak to my highest and best good.
10. …Direct all other energies to gently leave all parts of my body with grace and ease.
11. …Express deep, heartfelt gratitude to the animals and plants that offered themselves as sustenance to me.
12. …Express deep, heartfelt gratitude for the person who prepared the meal for me, even if I did it.

Personalizing the Guidelines to Optimize Digestion:

"I am implementing only what honors me"

Additional directives to create focus:

Suggested goals: to eat healthier, to get more enjoyment out of smart food choices, to appreciate your body and to heal an unhealthy relationship with food.

Your goal to achieve in association with these guidelines:

© Intentional Healing Systems, LLC

Exercising Personal Power

> *"If you realized how powerful your thoughts are,*
> *you would never think a negative thought."*
> —PEACE PILGRIM

The familiar word "willpower" suggests that the root words "will" and "power" have a relationship, which they do. Human beings have the divine right and ability to exercise free will. The course of a person's life is determined by the will they choose to lend power to and act upon. Every outcome is defined, on some level, by choice. This can be difficult to remember or even accept at times, but it is true.

Taking responsibility for our choices is a concept that has punitive overtones for many of us, probably as carryover from childhood. Often times as children when we "took responsibility" for our choices, we reaped consequences rather than rewards.

Consequences only represent one end of the spectrum of taking responsibility. Rewards represent the other, and when a person enjoys the rewards associated with taking ownership, the experience is incredibly empowering. Rewards give us reinforcement and help us believe that we have absolute power over the journey and in our ability to produce outcomes.

This list of intentions in the Exercising Personal Power Agreement aims to help subtly reconnect us with the memory that we are incredibly powerful. It serves as a subconscious training tool to remind us that we possess the ability to control the different aspects of our journey that contribute to final outcomes.

You can use this list of intentions to disconnect from a victim's mindset, feel more in control, and set clear boundaries with others.

17. Exercising Personal Power

I, ____________________, expect to…

1. …allow only situations that honor my highest good to manifest in my reality
2. …make choices that empower me
3. …remember that I have the ability to create favorable outcomes
4. …choose friends and partners who support me
5. …create situations that promote optimal physical and emotional comfort
6. …block energies that hinder my progress
7. …exercise self confidence
8. …set clear parameters with others and adhere to them
9. …manifest all changes with grace and ease
10. …connect only and always with a creator's mindset
11. …intentionally neutralize the energy of unfavorable thoughts I have by infusing them with energies based in love
12. …take responsibility for each day of my journey

Personalizing the Guidelines to Exercise Personal Power:

"I am in control"

Additional directives to create focus:

____

____

____

____

____

____

____

____

____

Suggested goals: feel more in control of your life, boost self-confidence, make choices that allow you to meet your goals with no resistance.

Your goal to achieve in association with these guidelines:

____

____

____

____

____

____

____

© Intentional Healing Systems, LLC

Instituting Joy

"Happiness is a perfume you cannot pour on others without getting some on yourself."
—Ralph Waldo Emerson

The beauty of life is displayed in the joy we experience. It is our birth right to claim as much joy as we can over the course of life but sometimes we forget the capacity we have to bring it into our lives.

Many times we participate in situations, relationships and exchanges that distract us from being truly happy. When we feel we are lacking happiness, we long for it. When we connect with lack in any way, we shut down our receptors that allow for receiving. On the other hand, we can keep those communication lines open if we direct our attention to the things that make us happy even in small ways.

Happiness only adds value to our lives. The energy of joy, as it is a direct descendant of love, can neutralize anger, hostility, and all by-products of fear. It also acts as energetic sustenance to foster growth of our wanted manifestations. When we feel happy, our inner light is amplified and we attract the energies that feed our desires.

A wonderful quality of joy, too, is that it is contagious. As you attract and exude joy, you provide an atmosphere for those around you to experience it with you. A group of joyous people together can amplify the energy of happiness in an exponential way with very little effort. Your joyous emanations carry with them untold riches that may reach farther than you ever could have imagined.

This set of intentions in the Instituting Joy Agreement can help you to stay centered in the quest for ever-present joy. It helps you to continually send out signals that purposely attract more opportunities for joy into your life.

18. Instituting Joy

I, ____________________, intend to…

1. …appreciate the beauty of nature
2. …create opportunities to laugh
3. …take time to do things that I really love to do
4. …redirect my thoughts to someone or something I love if I start to feel sad
5. …see the good in myself and others
6. …remain in harmony with other living beings
7. …live in the moment
8. …replace worries with confidence
9. …be content
10. …love my life
11. …smile often
12. …feel happy

Personalizing the Intentions to Institute Joy:

"I am happy"

Additional directives to create focus:

____

____

____

____

____

____

____

____

____

Suggested goals: be happy, appreciate the little things in life and help others to be happy.

Your goal(s) to achieve in association with these intentions:

____

____

____

____

____

____

____

Conclusion

The Agreements, Guidelines and Intentions laid out in this book pose an opportunity for you to create a step-by-step soul journey of awakening, healing and re-alignment of the inner and outer you.

You can follow the trail by using the information in the order it is delivered in the book, or you can create your own plan by focusing your attention on the Agreements, Guidelines and Intentions that speak to areas of personal development you wish to explore.

It is important to understand that this journey not only benefits you, but the entire collective consciousness (or all of humanity) benefits from your growth. Whenever you serve your highest good, you promote the greater good of all.

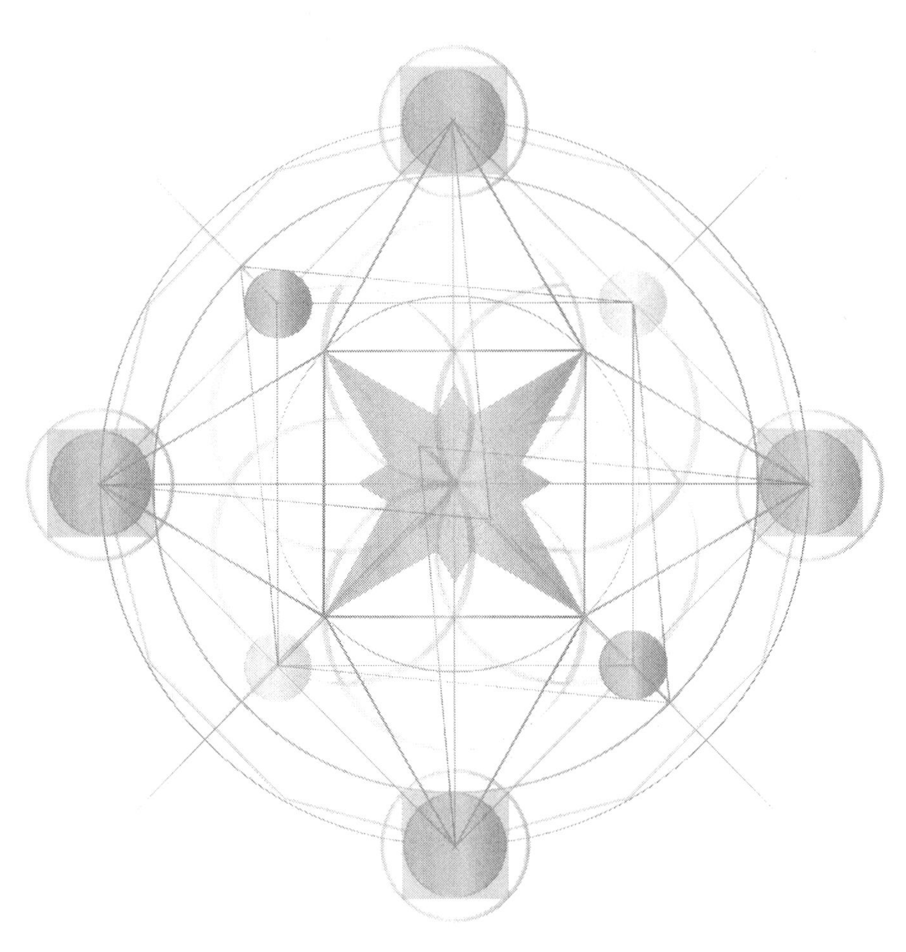

Acknowledgements

We are deeply grateful to our families and to our friends who supported us as we created this book.

The Teachings of Judy Cali, www.judycali.com

Transformational Life Mentoring of Leon van Kraayenburg, www.sacreddnakeys.com

Cover art and interior art contributions by Leon van Kraayenburg

The Teachings of Tantra Maat www.agencyofcreation.com

The Teachings of Paul J. Meyer

Leslie Hill, Certified Reiki Master/Reiki Teacher

Cover design and interior formatting by Tugboat Design

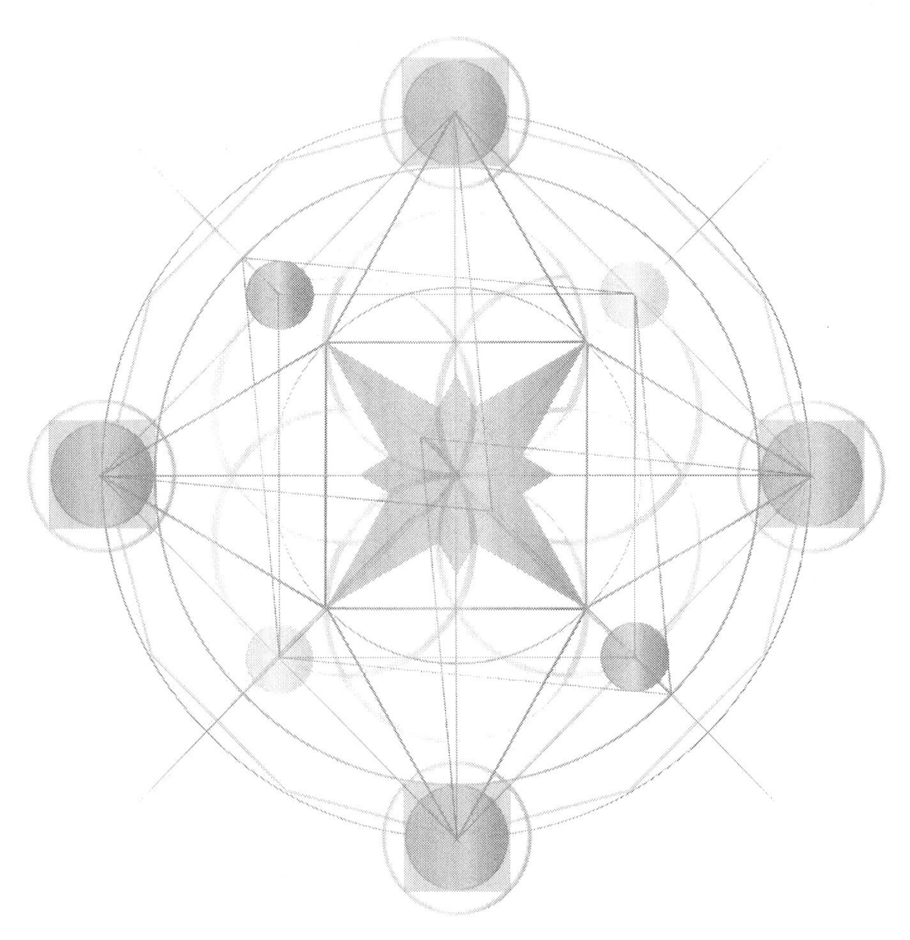

Glossary of Terms

Angels (your Angels) – the celestial beings that act as your guardians and watch over you at all times

Collective Consciousness – a group consciousness shared by all of humanity

Collective Humanity – humanity as a whole

Emanations – subtle energy output from the field around you

Emotional Independence – when a person is able to provide emotional sustenance to themselves rather than obtaining it from external sources

Energy Field – the measurable electrical field around your physical body

Guides (your guides) – the spiritual beings who offer guidance and support to you through your intuition

Higher Level Objectives – the goals of your soul

Higher Wisdom – the higher, all-knowing part of your soul

Inner Light – your soul

Law of Attraction – the magnetic, energetic force that brings similar energies together with one another

Light – energy, your energy output

Manifestation – an event or circumstance that has come to fruition

Manifested Goal – a goal that has been met

Masters – etheric beings of great spiritual wisdom and consciousness

Personal Power Center – the solar plexus, which governs your stomach and digestive track

Regenerative Energy – energy that flows without obstruction

Sacred Heart – the heart of your soul

Made in the USA
Middletown, DE
29 July 2023

35918129R00082